PUPPIES and KITTENS

by Nicole Corse

SCHOLASTIC INC.

New York   Toronto   London   Auckland
Sydney   Mexico City   New Delhi   Hong Kong

Puppies come in all shapes, colors, and sizes. There are over 150 different breeds of dogs in the world. But there is one thing they all have in common: They are totally adorable!

COCKER SPANIEL

There are about 40 different types of cats on planet Earth. Whether they are long-haired, short-haired, hairless, or somewhere in between, kittens are cuddly and cute!

NORWEGIAN FOREST CAT

An average mother dog typically gives birth to five to seven puppies in one litter. The size of the litter mostly depends on the size of the dog. For example, a bigger dog like the Labrador retriever can give birth to more than 15 puppies in the same litter.

LABRADOR RETRIEVER

A mother cat normally gives birth to two to four kittens in the same litter. In one year, a mother cat can give birth to three different litters. That's a lot of kittens!

ABYSSINIAN

During the first four weeks of their lives, puppies get all of their nutrients from their mother's milk. They do not need any other food to survive.

JACK RUSSELL TERRIER

During their first weeks of life, kittens rely only on their mom's milk for the nutrients they need to grow. The milk also helps protect them from getting sick.

SOMALI

At four weeks old, puppies can stop drinking milk and start eating solid food. To make the switch easier, most people soak the dry food with water for a few weeks.

BOSTON TERRIER

When kittens are between three and four weeks old, they can start eating moist kitten food. Each day kittens should be fed between four and six times.

Sometimes puppies will beg for food because it smells really good. But some human food can be dangerous to dogs, especially chocolate, avocados, onions, and grapes.

CHIHUAHUA

Some people think that kittens can drink milk and eat tuna fish, but these foods can harm a kitten. Milk from the grocery store can cause kittens to have stomach problems.

BiRMAN

A puppy's baby teeth start coming in at around three to four weeks old. Most puppies begin to grow permanent teeth when they are between four to six months old. During this time, puppies will chew on almost anything. Eventually, most puppies will grow 42 adult teeth.

GERMAN SHEPHERD

Kittens have about 26 baby teeth.
These teeth can be very sharp.
When a kitten is about three months
old, he or she will start to grow
permanent teeth. A cat has
30 adult teeth.

BURMESE

All dogs' tongues are pink except for the chow chow and Chinese shar-pei. Their tongues are black. Dogs have about 1,700 taste buds!

CHOW CHOW

Cats clean themselves with their tongues. Since a kitten can't lick her face and the top of her head, she licks her paws and then wipes them on the hard-to-reach places.

Puppies are born with their eyes
closed. When they are about 12 days
old, they start to open their eyes
and see the world around them.
It takes about a month for their eyes
to fully develop.

30

When kittens are born, their eyes are always blue. At around three months of age, a kitten may have a different eye color than the one it was born with!

BALINESE

Dogs bark, growl, whine, and howl to let humans know how they feel and to communicate with other dogs. A dog may bark because he or she is happy, lonely, warning someone of danger, or greeting a new person or dog.

BULLDOG

When kittens meow, they want their owner's attention. Kittens may feel hungry, cold, or maybe they just want to play! If a kitten hisses, it means he or she is angry and does not want to be played with.

MAINE COON

Dogs have over a million strands of fur that are constantly growing. Some dogs like the Bernese mountain dog shed a lot. Dogs like the poodle and shih tzu shed very little.

POODLE

Some cats have over a million strands of fur on their bodies. A Persian cat can grow fur up to eight inches long! The sphynx cat has very little hair on its body.

PERSIAN

Some puppies have long tails, some have short tails, and some have barely any tails at all! When puppies are happy, they wag their tails. When they are sad or scared, they will put their tails between their legs.

BEAGLE

A kitten's tail helps with balance, especially when walking on a difficult surface like the edge of a couch. If a kitten's tail is moving back and forth, it might be because the kitten is upset or angry.

RUSSIAN BLUE

Puppies have a lot of energy. It is important to give them the exercise they need. Puppies love to run around. The fastest dog is the greyhound. It can run up to 45 miles per hour.

GREYHOUND

Kittens sometimes get a burst of energy and will run around very fast. The fastest cat is the Egyptian mau. It can run over 30 miles per hour.

EGYPTIAN MAU

When dogs get hot, they will pant to cool themselves off and need to drink lots of water. Even though dogs are able to sweat through their noses and foot pads, it is much quicker for them to cool down by panting.

DALMATIAN

Kittens sweat through their paws.
If it is hot outside, kittens will lie
in the shade or the coolest spot
available. Make sure your kitten has
plenty of clean water to drink!

ORIENTAL

On average, a puppy sleeps about 15 to 20 hours each day. Sleeping is very important to a puppy's health especially since they are very active when they are awake.

PUG

Kittens love to play and explore, which makes them very tired. That's probably why kittens sleep so much! A kitten can sleep anywhere from 13 to 18 hours a day.

RAGDOLL

Puppies can start learning tricks
as early as eight weeks old. They
can learn to sit, lie down, beg, and
even give their owners a kiss!

GOLDEN RETRIEVER

Kittens have retractable claws. That means they can push their claws out or pull them in. In order to keep their claws sharp, kittens like to scratch things.

OCICAT

During the first weeks after a puppy is born, the puppy will learn about the world around him. The most important things for a puppy to do are to eat, sleep, and keep warm.

YORKiE

BERNESE MOUNTAIN DOG

Whether you like puppies, kittens, or both—these baby animals are totally adorable!

TURKISH ANGORA